Process

Process

www.GestaltNotebook.eu
© 2014 Stefan Green Meinel

Proofreading by Inge Tranter
Revised by David Kirk-Campbell

ISBN 978-87-711-4019-4
Second Edition

Manufacturer and publisher

Publisher: Books on Demand GmbH
Copenhagen, Denmark

Printer: Books on Demand GmbH
Norderstedt, Germany

Contents

Preface

Gestalt therapy is about process and immersion. You will sense, reflect, respond to and experiment with the relevant parts of your life situation. You can go far both emotionally and with regard to self-awareness.

The Gestalt approach is based on an open-minded study of context and self-expression. It is a process-oriented approach, which follows what is immediately meaningful and what instinctively feels right. You explore your feelings, draw conclusions and make decisions.

You leave the session affected by the work and with food for thought, but may have difficulty remembering all the insights you have gained – especially after some time has passed. The therapy will take effect anyway, but it is unfortunate that (possibly) hard-won and expensive personal work must be repeated several times, just because the content of the process drifts into the background. *Process* was developed with this situation in mind. It is designed to support and complement individual Gestalt therapy.

Process is a structured notebook with 77 pages for personal notes. It is divided into five chapters, each preceded by a short introduction and a series of cues and questions for inspiration. The chapters do not need to be written chronologically (although they have a logical sequence), but may be written according to relevance – freely skipping back and forth by writing (or drawing), following the content of the process.

You will benefit most from regular and structured writing. You will gain sharper focus, better overview and improved memory. Regular writing will deepen the effect of the therapy and improve the process of integration. The total course of therapy will go more smoothly and it is likely that it will assist in shortening the duration of the therapy.

Process works as a tool during the therapy. Afterwards – and later in life – the notebook will be a personal record of the work you did and the conditions and circumstances, you had to deal with.

This is not a notebook to be shared with anybody, and certainly not during the process of writing. It is a small piece of the soul, you should guard, and only share one day, after careful consideration, with people you think deserve your confidence.

Enjoy your notebook – good luck with the process!

Starting Point

All therapy has a *starting point*. The starting point is the life circumstances, issues and frustrations you want to deal with, that are the reasons you made contact with a Gestalt therapist.

The first prerequisite of the Gestalt therapeutic process is to explore, deepen and clarify the causes. The better you know the starting point the faster and more accurately you will be able to get to the work that facilitates real transformation.

This chapter is about becoming aware of *your* starting point. What are the circumstances that you want to deal with? Can you put it in a few sentences?

Once you know your starting point, you may want to elaborate a little bit. You might be inspired by the questions on the next page. How would you describe your situation? What is most important?

If your process at a later stage leads to work on other life circumstances, it will be to your advantage to return to this chapter and specify what it's about.

how does it affect you
what is it about
how much does it affect you
how does it feel
how long has it been going on
what **do you think**
how does your body react
what does your intuition tell you
what do you avoid
how do your surroundings react
how are you visible
who is it about

Direction

All therapy needs *direction*. Where should the process lead to? What do you want to achieve? The therapy may well be profound and powerful, but without direction you risk losing yourself in details and issues that might not really need treatment and attention.

The second prerequisite for the Gestalt therapeutic process is therefore to visualize and articulate the goal you want to achieve. It does not require vivid and expressive descriptions. The most important thing is that you can define your goals with some clarity, possibly in short and concise sentences.

What are *your* goals, *your* dreams and visions? Make room and space for this chapter. Give yourself plenty of time. Find a pleasant spot. Sit comfortably. What will make a positive change in your life? Which goals create a pleasant sensation inside you? What is your ultimate dream?

Your goals are like a compass, pointing the direction through the many options of the therapeutic process. Thus, you can benefit from returning to this chapter and checking whether your goals remained the same, whether to adjust or even to do a complete review. Let your hope speak – it will be an invaluable resource in your process.

the goal on the horizon

a good feeling within

Dreams

happy & satisfied within

I would like to do this

positive change

this is how I would like it to be

desire ● hope ● come into being

visions

Sessions

The two first chapters illustrate how a typical Gestalt therapeutic process begins. You take a look at the starting point and find a direction. With this in place, the therapy will be about *immersion*.

The therapy will alternate between conversations that generate insight and exercises that are carefully adapted to the needs and situation of the individual. You will get insight into your personal history, your patterns of reaction, your self-expression and your choices of action. You will search for meaningful explanations, see things from your own perspective and also in a larger context.

The exercises will most likely take place as *two chair work*, which is a brilliant tool to deal with things from the past as well as targeting experiments with self-expression and choices of action in an active way.

This chapter is used to write about the sessions, if possible immediately after they occurred so that the details are still fresh in your mind. What happened during the session? What were the most important insights? How did you react? What did you learn about yourself?

It will also be useful to make some notes about what you might want to work with next time, any comments you feel your therapist should hear about, and preferably also what you think worked well or maybe not so well (for you). Your feedback is important and always welcome.

emotional reactions
important insights
who is responsible for what
meaningful explanations
self-knowledge
reminders for the next session
my choices
decision process - inner context
what do I want - what do I do
two chair work

Observations

The therapy provides a safe environment to help you to take a stand regarding various events, to seek clarification and to make decisions – and to try out how you want to act in life. For a while, the process will have its axis in the immersion during the sessions, but gradually it will shift to the period *in between sessions* – to all of the occasions where you actively convert insight into action.

This chapter is about the experiences you have between sessions. What experiments have you made in your life? How did you feel inside? How did others around you react? What have you learned? What would you do differently next time?

Bring your writings to your therapy session, where you can get help to deal with and integrate your experiences plus get support and inspiration for the subsequent process.

It is important to remember that success does not depend on how well it went, or how others around you respond. It is a victory in itself that you even dared to set foot in new territory! Long term success depends on what you *learn* from your experiments.

Change can only be realized through *actual experience* with what is new and different. The more you learn about specific events the more competence you will get – and suddenly you will make small and large quantum leaps.

testing new behaviour

experiments

what happened - what did I learn

important experiences

my reactions - reactions from others

observations

what do my words and actions signal

how do I understand my surroundings

night dreams

reflections - realizations

Quantum Leaps

The purpose of the Gestalt therapeutic process is to create positive change. The final phase of the process is characterized by development of new competence. You are able to actively realize your goals in life. The sessions will usually take place with increasing intervals.

Change usually happens in small and large "quantum leaps" – all of a sudden you are *able to do it*. You feel differently and act differently – but often, you may paradoxically still question yourself in the same way as when the therapy began. It is characteristic that one of last things to change is your own self-image. The final phase of the process is usually about making room for joy regarding what is going well. Even good fortune must be integrated before the process is completed.

Thus, this chapter is about small and large moments of success. Make a note of when things are going well! It will help to integrate your new skills, and will make a decisive contribution towards adjusting your self-image. Furthermore, you may find it beneficial to go back and read how you described your starting point. What is different now? What changes have taken place?

If you have not already done so, it is a good time to talk about how and when the therapy should be terminated. The keystone of the process is your realization that you don't need therapy anymore. It is the moment when the status of this notebook changes from tool to valuable memory. When you can deservedly assign the therapy to the past and concentrate on enjoying the fruits of your labor!

this is how I did it
not a problem anymore
quantum leap
adjusting my self-image
suddenly I was able to
new competence
I finally said it
change on the inside
new horizons